GAIL GIBBONS
VOLCANOES

HOLIDAY HOUSE
NEW YORK

Library of Congress Cataloging-in-Publication Data
Names: Gibbons, Gail, author.
Title: Volcanoes! / Gail Gibbons.
Description: First edition. | New York : Holiday House, [2021]. | Audience:
Ages 4-8. | Audience: Grades 2-3. | Summary: "A nonfiction primer on all
things volcanoes, including the different types of volcanoes, the work of
volcanologists, and more"— Provided by publisher.
Identifiers: LCCN 2019045735 | ISBN 9780823445691 (hardcover)
Subjects: LCSH: Volcanoes—Juvenile literature. | Plate tectonics—Juvenile
literature. | Earth sciences—Juvenile literature.
Classification: LCC QE521.3 .G495 2021 | DDC 551.21—dc23
LC record available at https://lccn.loc.gov/2019045735

ISBN: 978-0-8234-4569-1 (hardcover)

The publisher would like to thank Dr. Einat Lev, Lamont Associate Research
Professor and leader of the physical volcanology group at Columbia
University's Lamont–Doherty Earth Observatory,
for checking this book for scientific accuracy.

VOLCANO
EVACUATION
ROUTE

The top of a volcano is its SUMMIT.

VOLCANO

The word VOLCANO comes from the name of the ancient Roman god of fire, VULCAN.

The ground begins to rumble. Loud roars, hissing, and violent blasts are coming from deep inside the Earth. Suddenly ash, hot lava and rock, and gases shoot up into the air. Then hot molten lava flows down the volcano's sides.

OUTER CORE

← 1,400 miles
(2,200 kilometers)
thick →

INNER CORE

← 1,500 miles
(2,400 kilometers)
thick →

Earth is made up of four layers. The inner core is a hot ball of solid iron and nickel. The outer core is made up of hot liquid iron and nickel.

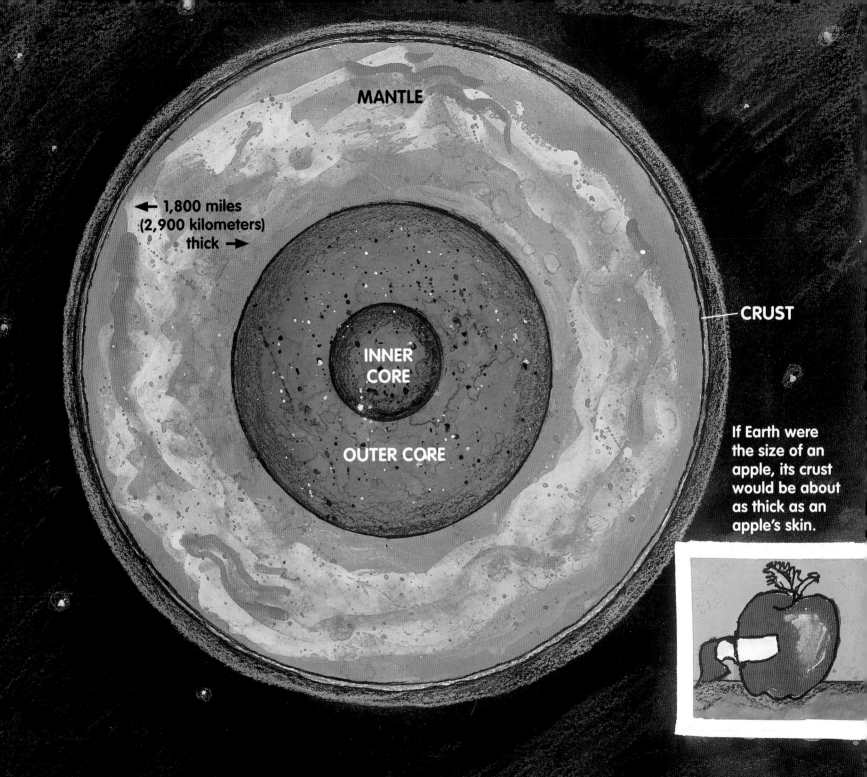

MANTLE

← 1,800 miles
(2,900 kilometers)
thick →

CRUST

INNER CORE

OUTER CORE

If Earth were
the size of an
apple, its crust
would be about
as thick as an
apple's skin.

The third section, called the mantle, surrounds the outer core. It is mostly solid rock. The outer edge of the mantle is softer and moves slowly. The fourth section is called the crust. It is a very thin layer of rock and soil. It is where we live.

LAVA

LAYERS of ash, lava, and other
materials are called STRATA.

MAGMA

CRACK! Volcanoes erupt when an opening develops in Earth's crust,
and hot molten rock from the mantle, called magma, is forced through
the crack.

The MANTLE'S temperature
is about 6,000°F inside.

6

VOLCANOLOGY is the study of volcanoes.

COMPUTER DATA

GAS MONITOR

THERMAL IMAGERS measure heat.

SEISMOMETERS detect movements in the Earth.

TILT METERS measure the angle of a volcano.

The volcanic explosivity index (VEI) is a strength scale ranging from 0 to 8.

Volcanologists study volcanoes. They believe most of Earth's crust is between 6 and 30 miles (10 to 50 kilometers) thick. They can measure the magnitude and strength of a volcanic eruption using special instruments. They can sometimes predict whether or not an eruption will occur.

7

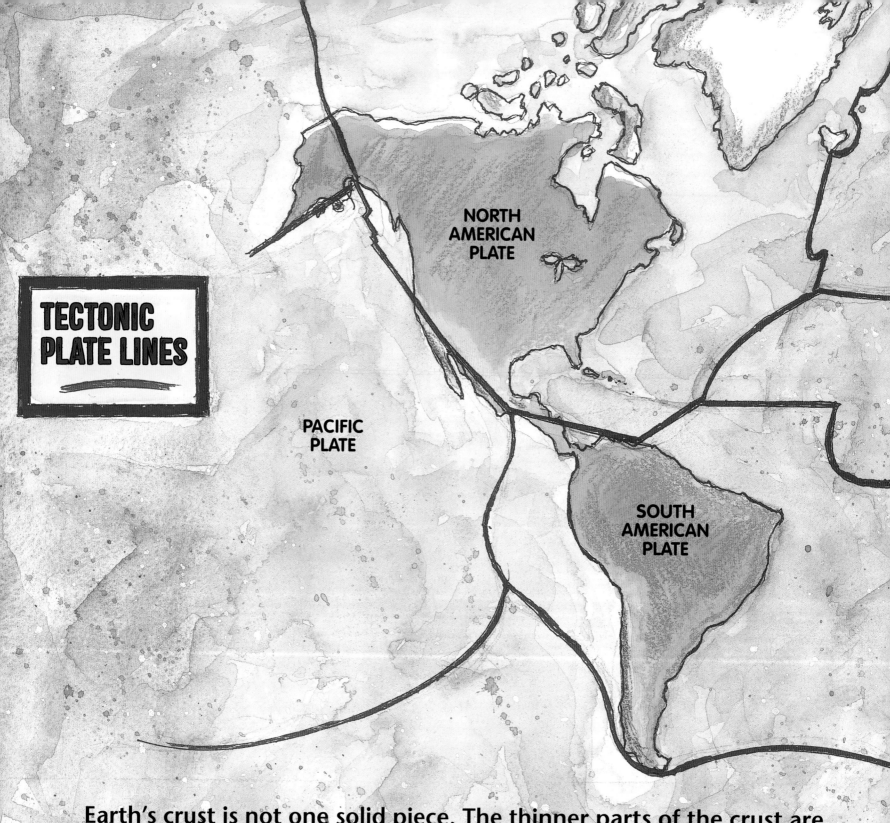

TECTONIC PLATE LINES

NORTH AMERICAN PLATE

PACIFIC PLATE

SOUTH AMERICAN PLATE

Earth's crust is not one solid piece. The thinner parts of the crust are most likely to develop openings that will become volcanoes.

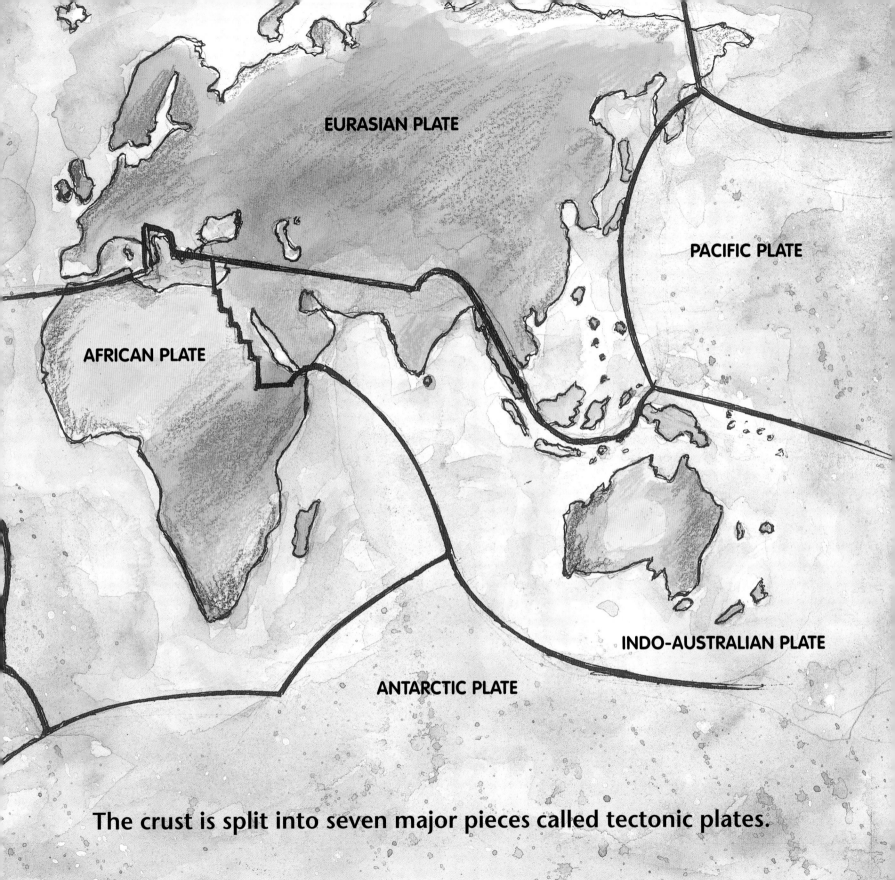

EURASIAN PLATE

PACIFIC PLATE

AFRICAN PLATE

INDO-AUSTRALIAN PLATE

ANTARCTIC PLATE

The crust is split into seven major pieces called tectonic plates.

ANTARCTICA

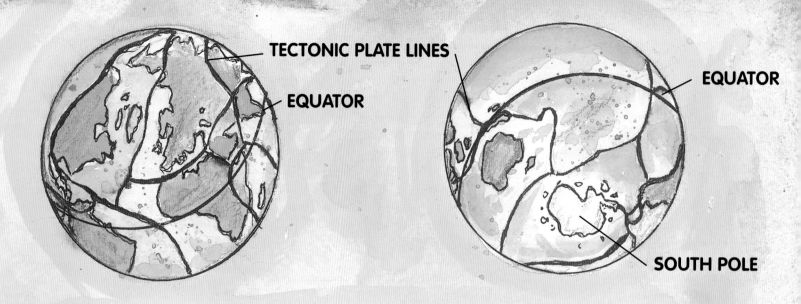

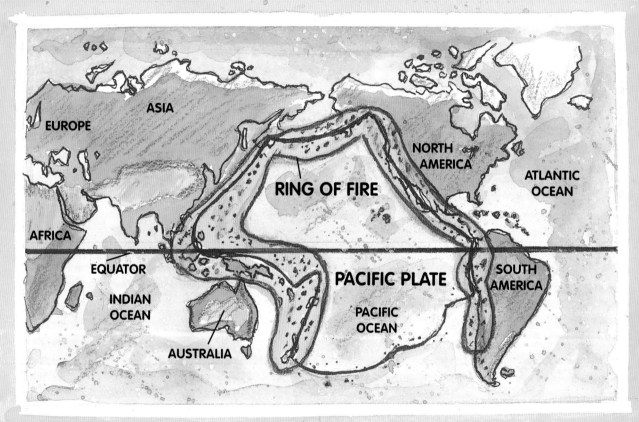

The tectonic plates fit together around Earth like a jigsaw puzzle. Most volcanoes are on or near the edges of the plates. One plate, the Pacific Plate, has more than half of Earth's volcanoes around its edges, in what is called the "ring of fire."

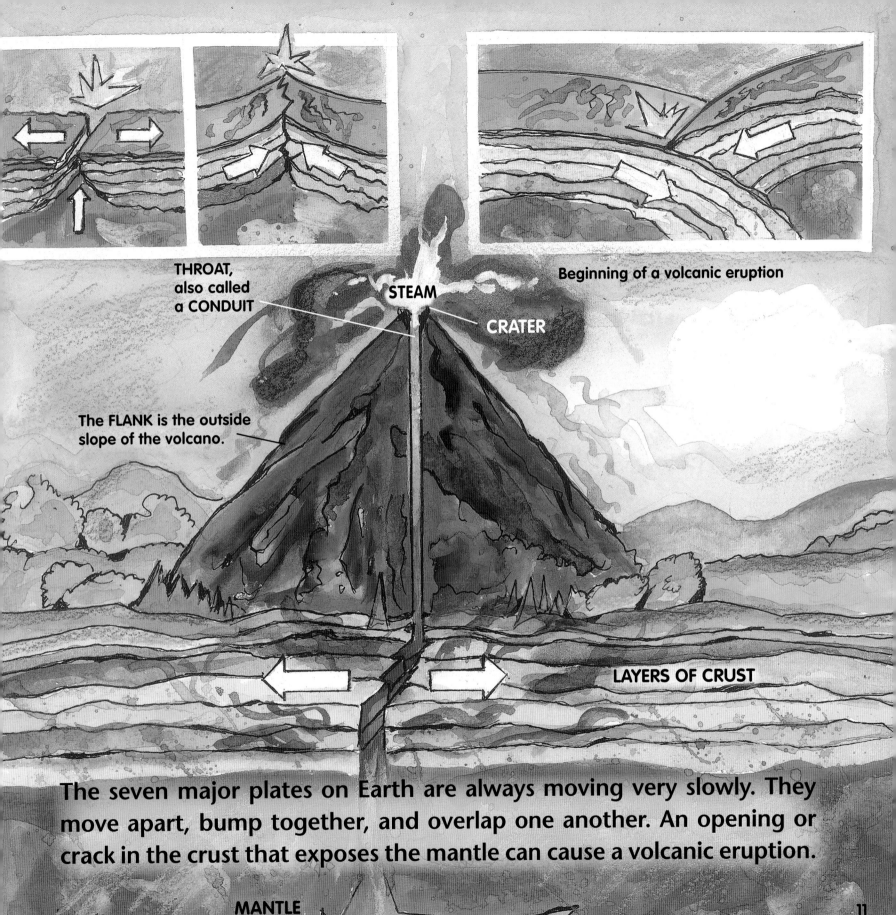

THROAT, also called a CONDUIT

STEAM

CRATER

Beginning of a volcanic eruption

The FLANK is the outside slope of the volcano.

LAYERS OF CRUST

The seven major plates on Earth are always moving very slowly. They move apart, bump together, and overlap one another. An opening or crack in the crust that exposes the mantle can cause a volcanic eruption.

MANTLE

MAGMA

TYPES OF VOLCANOES
SHIELD VOLCANO

Some SHIELD VOLCANOES can be very tall.

CRATER

DUST

STEAM

LAVA

VENT

CRATER

VENT

VENT

VENT

LAVA FLOWS

MAGMA

LAYERS of CRUST

In this type of volcano, lava flows slowly from vents and spreads outward, sometimes for miles. A series of lava flows builds up over time into a low, broad shape that looks like a shield.

MAGMA

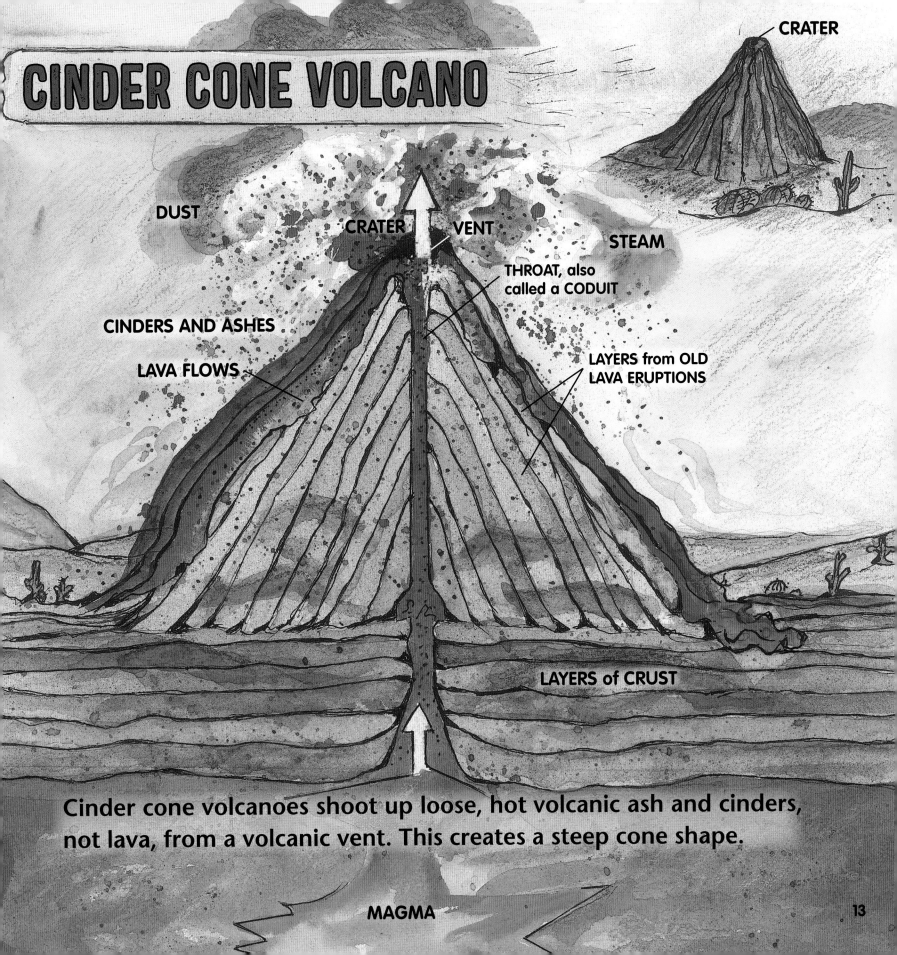

CINDER CONE VOLCANO

CRATER

DUST

CRATER VENT

STEAM

THROAT, also called a CODUIT

CINDERS AND ASHES

LAVA FLOWS

LAYERS from OLD LAVA ERUPTIONS

LAYERS of CRUST

Cinder cone volcanoes shoot up loose, hot volcanic ash and cinders, not lava, from a volcanic vent. This creates a steep cone shape.

MAGMA

LAVA DOME VOLCANO

CRATER

CRATER

VENT

LAVA

DOME VOLCANOES are often small.

HARDENED LAVA

LAYERS OF CRUST

Lava dome volcanoes send up extremely viscous lava that hardens into a dome shape. They usually only erupt one time.

MAGMA

14

COMPOSITE VOLCANO
ALSO CALLED A STRATOVOLCANO

CRATER
CONE SUMMIT

CRATER
CONE SUMMIT
VENT

LAVA

The FLANK is the outside slope of the volcano.

LAYERS from old ash eruptions

A composite volcano forms over hundreds of thousands of years and many eruptions. The eruptions build up layers thousands of feet tall. Some layers are old, hardened lava. Other layers can be made up of ash, rock, and other materials.

LAYERS OF CRUST

MAGMA

15

ERUPTION OF A LARGE COMPOSITE VOLCANO

DUST

CRATER   VENT

THROAT, also called a CONDUIT

MAGMA

The FLANK is the outside slope of the volcano.

LAYERS from old ash eruptions

The ground around a composite volcano's base begins to rumble and shake. Underneath the Earth's crust, two tectonic plates push together, causing intense pressure. Magma, gases, ash, and rocks force their way up from deep inside the volcano. The volcano is about to erupt.

MAGMA   COLLIDING PLATES

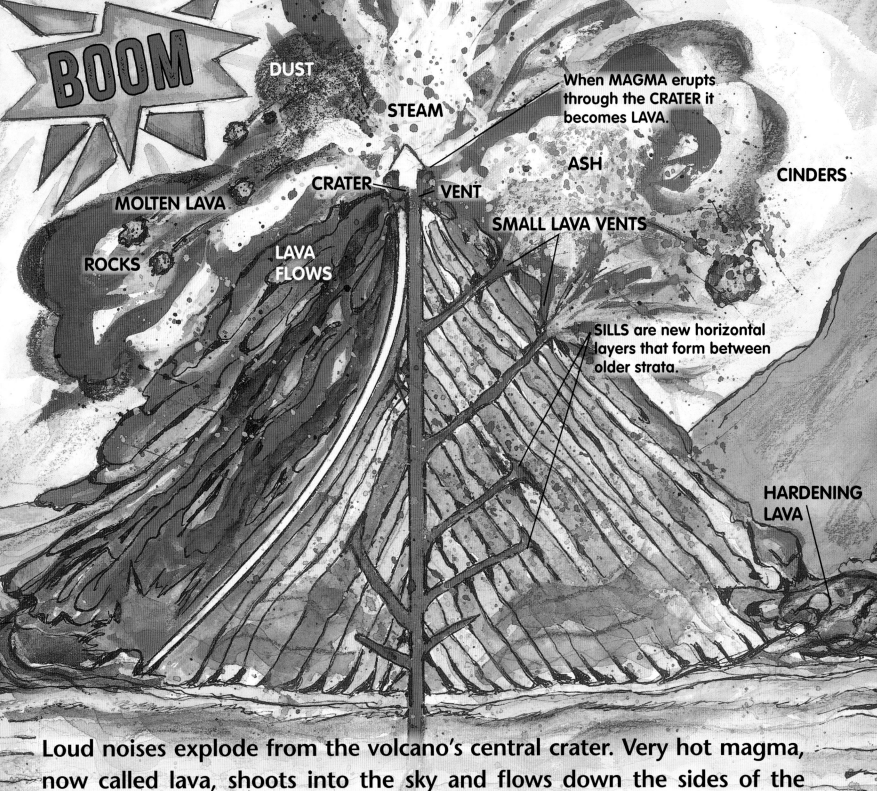

Loud noises explode from the volcano's central crater. Very hot magma, now called lava, shoots into the sky and flows down the sides of the volcano in streams. Rocks, ash, steam, gases, and dust also burst into the air from the crater. Such an explosion can destroy life for many miles around.

UNDERWATER VOLCANOES

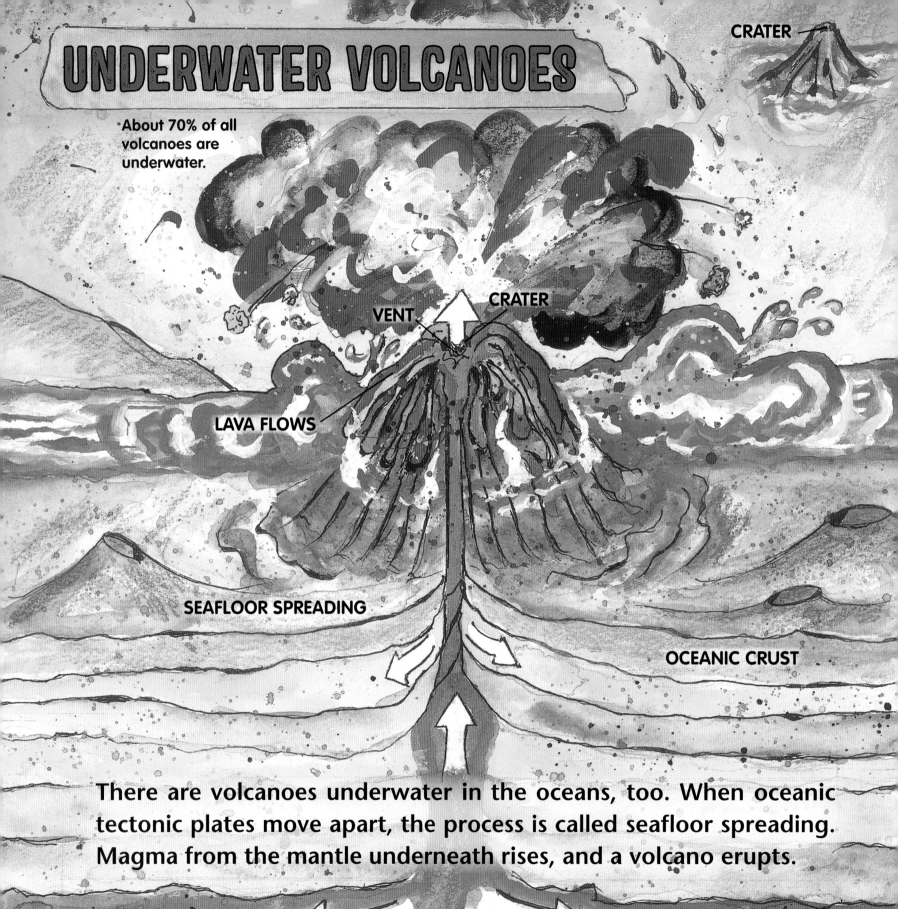

CRATER

About 70% of all volcanoes are underwater.

VENT

CRATER

LAVA FLOWS

SEAFLOOR SPREADING

OCEANIC CRUST

There are volcanoes underwater in the oceans, too. When oceanic tectonic plates move apart, the process is called seafloor spreading. Magma from the mantle underneath rises, and a volcano erupts.

SEAFLOOR MAGMA

TOP EDGE OF MANTLE'S MAGMA

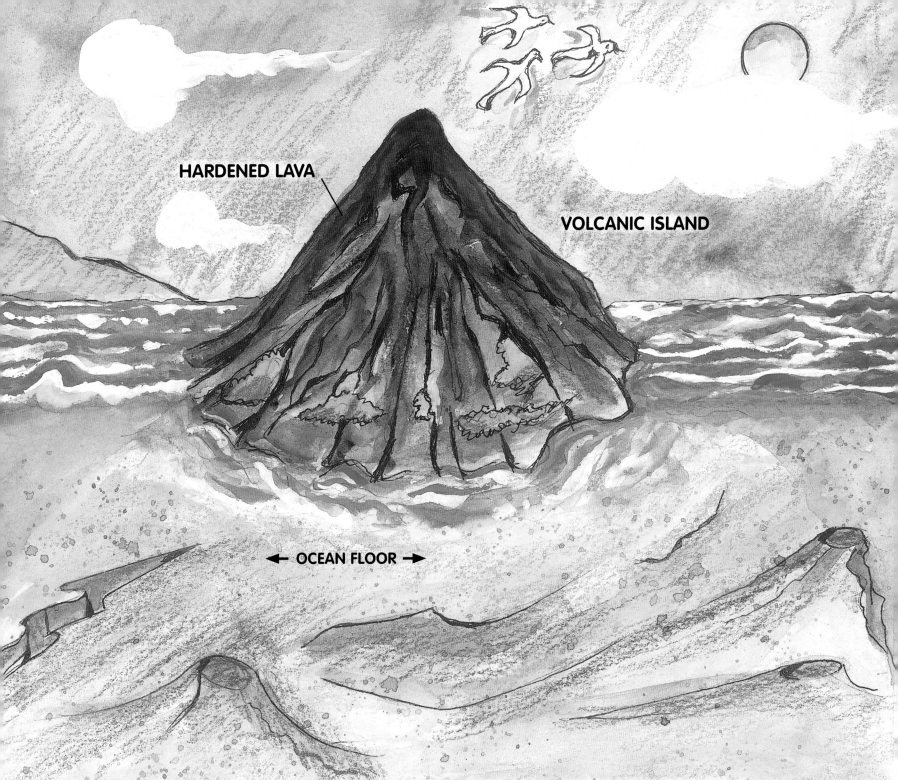

HARDENED LAVA

VOLCANIC ISLAND

← OCEAN FLOOR →

When the magma cools, it becomes hard. As the same volcano erupts over and over, layers build up. The underwater volcano becomes taller and taller. When it rises above sea level, it can become an island.

DUST

ASH

CINDERS

MOLTEN LAVA

MOLTEN LAVA ROCKS
Also called
LAVA BOMBS

LAVA FLOWS

The volcano's eruption can destroy anything in its way. It is dangerous for people and animals. Hot gases, ash, lava, and rocks are destructive. Volcanoes can also cause earthquakes.

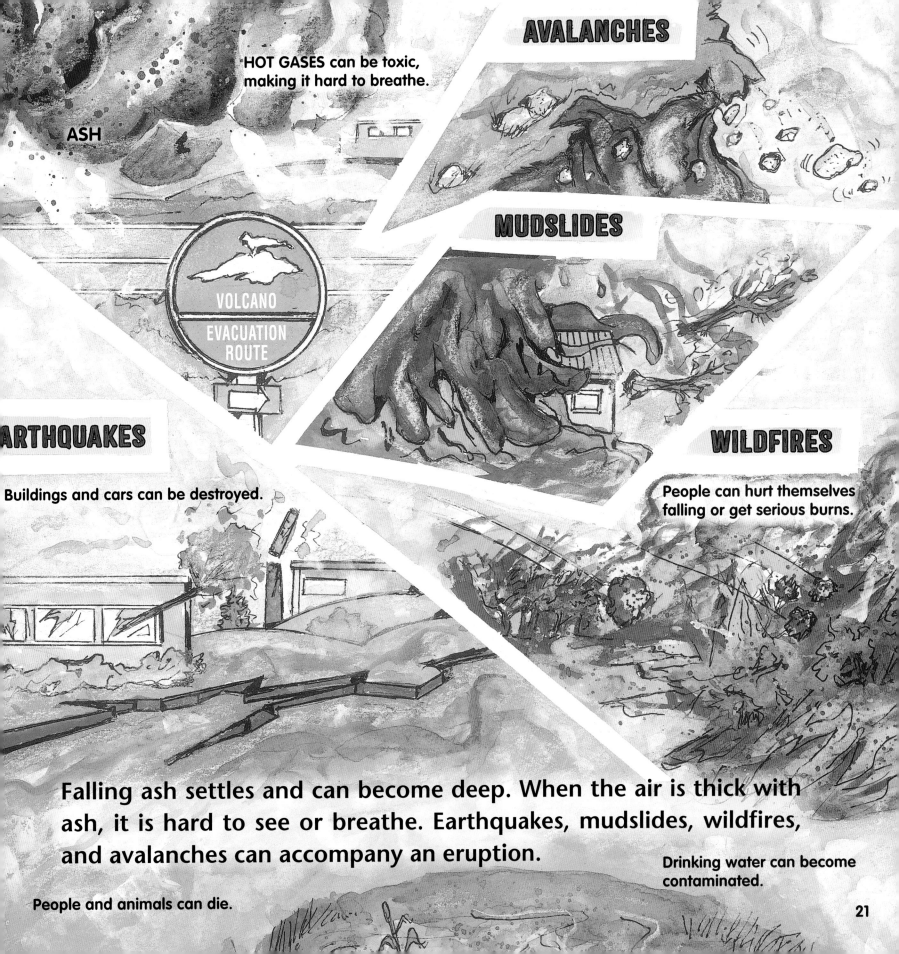

HOT GASES can be toxic, making it hard to breathe.

ASH

AVALANCHES

VOLCANO
EVACUATION
ROUTE

MUDSLIDES

EARTHQUAKES

Buildings and cars can be destroyed.

WILDFIRES

People can hurt themselves falling or get serious burns.

Falling ash settles and can become deep. When the air is thick with ash, it is hard to see or breathe. Earthquakes, mudslides, wildfires, and avalanches can accompany an eruption.

Drinking water can become contaminated.

People and animals can die.

WHAT TO DO WHEN THERE IS A VOLCANIC WARNING

1. Listen for emergency information and siren alerts.

2. Follow evacuation orders right away if they are given.

3. Avoid land that slopes down from a volcano.

4. Wear protective clothing and sturdy shoes.

5. NEVER drive in heavy ash falls.

6. Have a survival kit with you that includes food, bottled water, a flashlight with extra batteries, goggles, and a respirator mask.

7. Go to a designated shelter if you are told to.

SHELTER

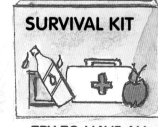

SURVIVAL KIT

TRY TO HAVE AN ADULT HELP YOU.

Some people donate money and supplies.

Volunteers come to help.

After the volcanic eruption is over, be careful. Wait until it is safe to go outside. Often organizations and volunteers come to help people and assist in a cleanup plan.

23

FAMOUS VOLCANOES

Kilauea in Hawaii is an ACTIVE VOLCANO.

A volcano is ACTIVE if it has erupted within the last 10,000 years.

PACIFIC OCEAN

HAWAII

KILAUEA

Volcanoes are classified as active, dormant, or extinct. Active volcanoes have regular activity. Some erupt constantly.

SEA OF JAPAN

JAPAN

MOUNT FUJI

PACIFIC OCEAN

Devil's Tower in Wyoming is an EXTINCT VOLCANO. It's about 50 million years old.

EXTINCT VOLCANO

DORMANT VOLCANO

Mount Fuji in Japan is a DORMANT VOLCANO.

DEVIL'S TOWER

WYOMING

Dormant volcanoes may not erupt for long periods of time, but volcanologists know they can erupt again. An extinct volcano will never erupt again.

MOUNT VESUVIUS

POMPEII

ADRIATIC SEA

ITALY

TYRRHENIAN SEA

SICILY

IONIAN SEA

MOUNT VESUVIUS

POMPEII

Pompeii was buried under 13 to 20 feet (4 to 6 meters) of ash.

Archaeologists study how people lived in Pompeii.

About two thousand years ago, the Mount Vesuvius volcano near Pompeii, Italy, suddenly erupted. Ash quickly covered the city. During the 1700s archaeologists began uncovering the ruins of Pompeii. They were very surprised. Some parts of buildings, roads, other structures, and also shapes of people, were found when ash was removed. These were all preserved by the volcanic eruption. Pompeii is still being excavated.

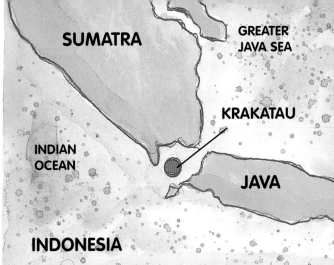

SUMATRA

GREATER JAVA SEA

KRAKATAU

INDIAN OCEAN

JAVA

INDONESIA

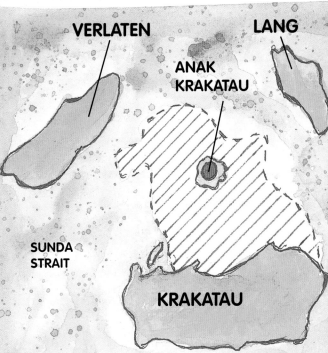

VERLATEN

LANG

ANAK KRAKATAU

SUNDA STRAIT

KRAKATAU

Krakatau is still active but not as powerful.

The Krakatau volcano in Indonesia erupted in 1883. It was one of the largest eruptions in modern times. The volcano is on an island between Sumatra and Java. After the volcano erupted, only one-third of the island was left. About 165 villages were destroyed. At least 36,500 people died.

CANADA

WASHINGTON STATE

PACIFIC OCEAN

MOUNT ST. HELENS

OREGON

ACTIVE VOLCANO

MUDFLOW

In 1980 the Mount St. Helens volcano in the state of Washington erupted. It created the largest landslide ever recorded. It was the most destructive volcanic eruption in United States history.

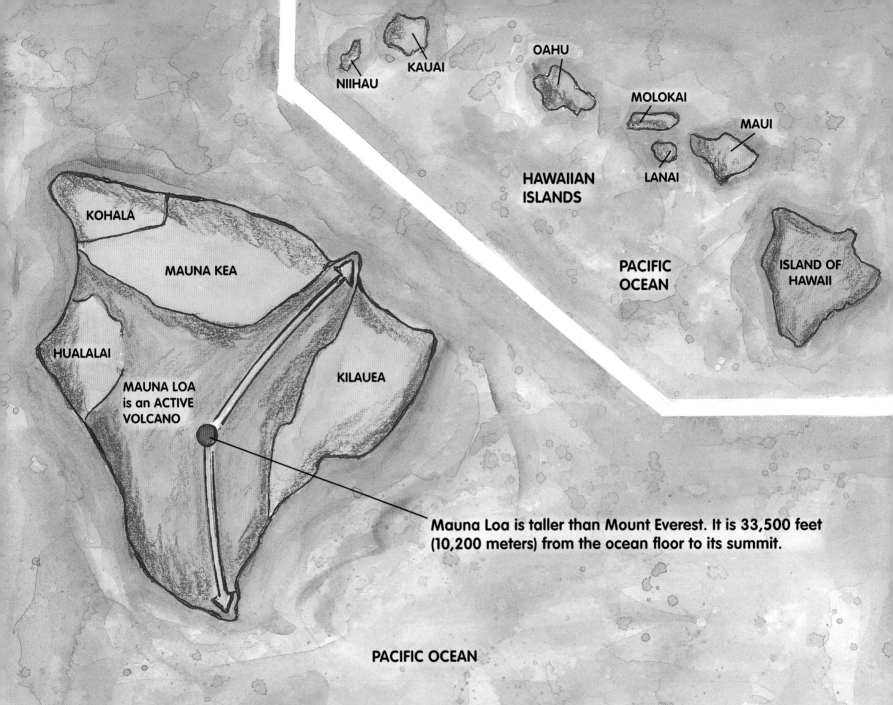

KAUAI

NIIHAU

OAHU

MOLOKAI

MAUI

HAWAIIAN
ISLANDS

LANAI

PACIFIC
OCEAN

ISLAND OF
HAWAII

KOHALA

MAUNA KEA

HUALALAI

KILAUEA

MAUNA LOA
is an ACTIVE
VOLCANO

Mauna Loa is taller than Mount Everest. It is 33,500 feet
(10,200 meters) from the ocean floor to its summit.

PACIFIC OCEAN

The world's largest volcano is in Hawaii. Its name is Mauna Loa, which means "long mountain." It stretches 74 miles (120 kilometers), from the southern tip of the island of Hawaii to the northeast coastline near the city of Hilo. All of the Hawaiian Islands were formed by volcanoes.

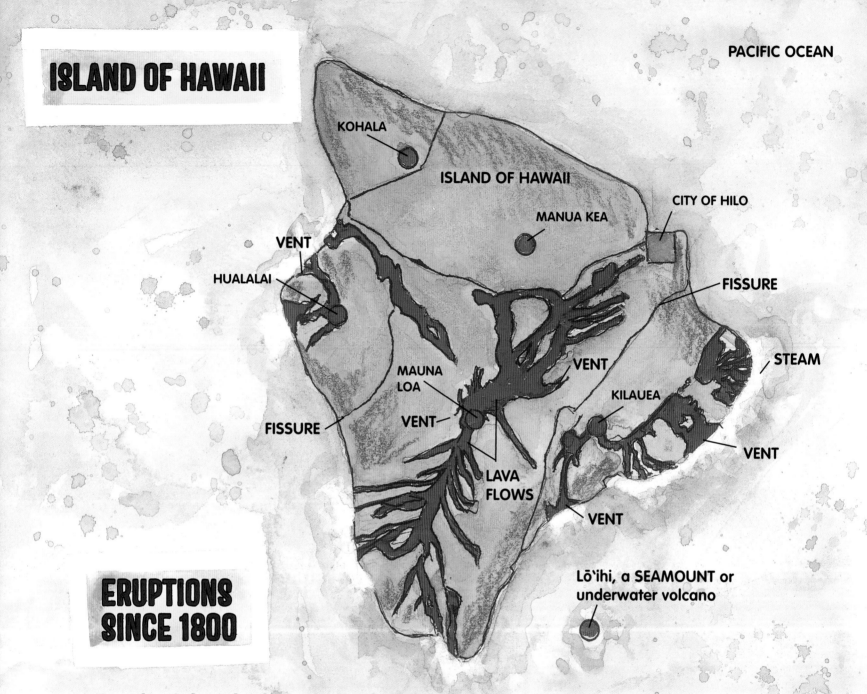

ISLAND OF HAWAII

KOHALA

ISLAND OF HAWAII

MANUA KEA

CITY OF HILO

VENT

HUALALAI

FISSURE

STEAM

MAUNA LOA

VENT

KILAUEA

FISSURE

VENT

VENT

LAVA FLOWS

VENT

Lōʻihi, a SEAMOUNT or underwater volcano

ERUPTIONS SINCE 1800

On the island of Hawaii, there are a number of volcanoes and many vents. There are also volcanic fissures that extend all the way to the shoreline and have destroyed homes. When the lava hits the ocean, it hardens, making the island bigger.

NEVER go sightseeing where there is an active volcano without a qualified guide.

Some people travel to see volcanoes. They should have guides to protect them from any dangers. Park rangers, volcanologists, and other people who have experience around volcanoes must take charge. Volcanoes can be dangerous. It's amazing to see and learn about volcanoes. Remember to respect them. Earth, and volcanoes along with it, is always changing.

VOLCANO FACTS

Between 10 and 30 volcanoes are erupting somewhere on Earth every day.

There are about 1,500 volcanoes on land that are known to have been active.

The temperature of hot lava can range from 1,300°F to 2,200°F (700°C to 1,200°C).

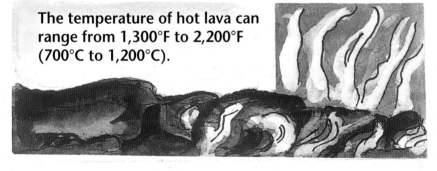

There are about 350 million people living within danger zones where a volcano could become active.

A CALDERA is a collapsed cone. Sometimes a lake might form at the bottom of it.

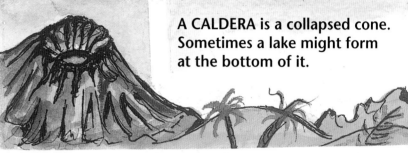

Volcanoes can cause earthquakes that can create huge waves called TSUNAMIS. They can cause terrible damage to people and their homes.

When hot lava flows, it glows from hot white to red. When it cools and hardens, it turns black.

Over time, pressures on hardened lava rocks will turn them into different kinds of rocks.